PRIMERS

Volume Six

PRIMERS

Volume Six

To Ahina

Kym Deyn
Estelle Price
Fathima Zahra

from

Nine
Arches
Press

Primers: Volume Six
Kym Deyn, Estelle Price, and Fathima Zahra
Selected by: Rishi Dastidar and Jane Commane

ISBN: 978-1-913437-44-2
eBook ISBN: 978-1-913437-45-9

First published June 2022 by:

Nine Arches Press
Unit 14, Sir Frank Whittle Business Centre,
Great Central Way, Rugby.
CV21 3XH
United Kingdom

www.ninearchespress.com

Nine Arches Press is supported using public funding
by Arts Council England.

About the Selecting Editors:

Rishi Dastidar is a fellow of The Complete Works, a consulting editor at *The Rialto* magazine, a member of Malika's Poetry Kitchen, and chair of writer development organisation Spread The Word. A poem from his debut collection *Ticker-tape* was included in *The Forward Book of Poetry 2018*, and his second collection, *Saffron Jack*, was published in the UK by Nine Arches Press in 2020. He is also editor of *The Craft: A Guide to Making Poetry Happen in the 21st Century* (Nine Arches Press), and co-editor of *Too Young, Too Loud, Too Different: Poems from Malika's Poetry Kitchen* (Corsair).

Jane Commane is a poet, editor and publisher. Her first full-length collection, *Assembly Lines,* was published by Bloodaxe in 2018. A graduate of the Warwick Writing Programme, in 2016 she was chosen to join Writing West Midlands' Room 204 writer development programme. Jane is editor at Nine Arches Press, co-editor of *Under the Radar* magazine, and is co-author, with Jo Bell, of *How to Be a Poet,* a creative writing handbook (Nine Arches Press). In 2017, she was awarded a Jerwood Compton Poetry Fellowship.

Contents

Fathima Zahra

FOREWORD

The Primers poetry mentoring scheme began in 2015 with the intention of seeking out and supporting exciting poetry by a range of debut poets. Primers runs biannually and has now published nineteen new poets, with three finalists each time selected by a guest judge and receiving one-to-one mentoring and editing advice, all designed to take their poetry into print and out into the world.

The 2021 call for submissions brought us an invigorating selection of new writing. In reading through these submissions, we were able to take a sample of the poetic waters and of the many talented new poets out there.

There is of course nothing more exciting in reading poetry than finding a voice new to you, and feeling *that* feeling – where the brain says 'oh hello, what have we here?', as the skin responds with a tingle and your face starts smiling as you realise, *there is something special in these words.*

That, roughly described, was our initial sensation on seeing the work of Kym Deyn, Estelle Price and Fathima Zahra. Each, in their unique ways, have that uncanny ability to recast what you thought you knew, as they make you look then look again at who we are, how we live, and what we might be.

Kym Deyn's work is startling in its originality. Their poems open out into a world of magic and mourning, where conversations with faerie children, bog bodies, and those who have crossed over into the spirit world are standard, where reality is hazy in the way the best summer evenings are, and where enchantment isn't a possibility but a command; the past, present, now-life and afterlife meet in Deyn's poems which are formally and thematically audacious and bold.

Estelle Price's dextrous work is driven by a keen ear, fastidiously sculpting memory, experience, and language into a series of compelling moments examining power and status under patriarchy. That makes the poems sound dry: far from it, there is an easy and pleasing intimacy here too, one which is unafraid of allowing poems to slip seamlessly into a variety of forms which reflect the dynamic momentum of their narratives – and of life itself.

Fathima Zahra's work is brilliantly simple in its appearance on the surface. Beware, for underneath there lurks a cunning wit and a sharp eye for an image that lingers in the memory. Together they form poems that both show the difficulty of fitting in, and the strength that comes from not doing so. Zahra's unique and illuminating voice has the perfect touch for tuning in to the distinctive closeness of girlhood and womanhood's conversations and secrets within her richly-rewarding and precise lines.

Getting to know Kym, Estelle and Fathima through the mentoring process has been a pleasure. This work can be radical and difficult, as writers start to explore the outer edges of their ability and ambition, answering questions about what they are trying to do at the level of an individual line or word – but also about the dent they want to leave on the face of the world. All three have embraced this process with a rare aplomb.

All three poets also impressed us with their determination and enthusiasm, and we are so pleased to have been part of their journey towards publication. Our thanks also to the seven other shortlisted poets: Jenny Danes, Juliet Humphreys, Oli Isaac, Dillon Jaxx, Prerana Kumar, Sally Tissington, and Sammy Weaver, whose memorable and skilful poems we also enjoyed. We hope that a Primers shortlisting has been a valuable recognition of your poems, and we extend our thanks to the longlisted poets whose new writing also caught our eye.

We're thrilled at what you're about to read, and we are delighted to bring these three wonderful poets and their work to you. Just wait for *that feeling*.

Rishi Dastidar and Jane Commane,
Selecting Editors, *Primers Volume Six*

June 2022

Kym Deyn

Kym Deyn is a poet, playwright and fortune teller. They have a *Legitimate Snack* forthcoming with Broken Sleep Books, as well as work in Carcanet's Brotherton Poetry Prize Anthology. Otherwise, they have been widely published in a range of anthologies and journals including *Butcher's Dog* and the *Valley Press Anthology of Prose Poetry*. They are one of the winners of the 2020 Outspoken Prize for Poetry.

Guide for Passage Into St. Martin's Land

1.) Find a paper map, earth splayed like cut fruit. Turn it over. Here is the blank page, impossible task, fictitious geography.

2.) Then walk backwards using your compass as a pendulum.

3.) Stand in doorways with your foot in a bucket of water.

4.) Split your face like Janus.

5.) Fall laughing backwards over the edge of a cliff.

6.) Wear a hagstone like a monocle.

7.) Stand on the beach at twilight, threshold of day and night, land and sea.

8.) Ask yourself if the sea and the sky can switch places, if there are endless possible reflections in mirrors, if the horizon is a line you can dance on, if the moon is hung in the sky with string, if your laughter is a ticker tape parade, if there's magic if there's magic if there's magic if there's magic

        8a.) If there's magic, can you step off the underside of the map and arrive all at once?

Note: In the 12th century, two green children (a brother and sister) were found outside the Sussex village of Woolpit, they spoke a strange language, and at first would eat only broad beans. The girl survived and her colour faded. She learned English and claimed to have come from the subterranean St Martin's Land.

My Girlfriend Came From St. Martin's Land

She brushes her teeth and pulls a single leaf from her ear. We never talk about it. The green vanished with her baptism, she learned to eat foods other than broad beans, forgot her own words for home. I ask her if she misses her brother and she says, *like a grafted branch misses its first tree, like a tooth misses a mouth*. I never knew her before, the colour of a fresh pear. I'm dreaming her face unfurling into leaves, skin sprouting moss. I see her reflection in the bathroom mirror, a green girl with sharp teeth. I caught her chewing the stems of house plants, trying to pick the chlorophyll from kale, bathing in olives. I ask her if she wants to go home, she says nothing, lifts her tongue. The underneath is green green green

Rumours Concerning the Green Children of Woolpit

Are they foriegn?   Not just Foriegn, Mary, look at them!   Are they sick?
Do they speak English?   You're frightening them!   You
there, girl, say something. ⸤᚛unintelligible script᚜⸥ *What is that? French?*
French, Robert, are you thick?   Have some care for fuck's sake,
they're children. ⸤᚛unintelligible script᚜⸥ *With a language like that*
maybe they've come from Hell.
Are they very strange?   Very!   They're faeries of course   or
creatures dressed up in human skin.   I swear the girl's colour is fading by
the day. She's almost pretty.   You've stopped them speaking that awful
tongue?   Won't have it in the house.   St Martin? Our St. Martin?
A country of mist.   The boy cries at midday. Flinches at bread.   I
heard they have chicken tongues, cloven hooves.   I heard they hate iron
and spit on the cross.   Do you think you could go there?   Where?
*   That land of theirs.*
Pity about the boy. He was baptised at least. The girl cried ⸤᚛unintelligible script᚜⸥
over and over.   Poor mite.   She said her father was a lord.   Said they walked
out of a cave mouth.   We never found the way.   If it existed it all.
*   Magic maybe.   An act of God.   She became a wanton little thing didn't she?*
Is it true?   Any of it?   Every word.
None of it.   I asked her once and she just said: ⸤᚛unintelligible script᚜⸥

my brother and I went walking in our father's lands through the cow pastures, the broad hedgerows, the rabbit's dens, there was a thick mist covering the cave's roof the stalagmites peaked through like strangely up-side down mountains they dripped and we played a game of dancing between drips we saw a stag with a thorny crown in the dist-ance then bells started clashing we were so afraid and when we finally open-ed our eyes we saw for the first time an open sky

Main Cities of St Martin's Land

Delilah where we grow roses the colour of mist.
Rusk where the potters go mad and glaze the streets.

Sulyard sits on the edge of a subterranean sea, lit
by the green glow of the horizon at twilight.

Our capital is Pook, city of walled gardens,
jewelled guildhalls, guarded by the out-of-sights,
the St-Martin's-Helpers, the trisksy-wisps.

Urswick, built during the war, keeps many
houses inside the tottering walls, some say
whole gardens, fishponds, tennis courts.

Brayles is a university city, where sages
debate what stones glint in the dark above,
dissect the creatures from the lightless sea,
dream of the Unsubmerged Lands.

Veneer lies on our border with Elphame,
a hedge where a light peers through
an extraordinary market surrounds it
where faeries sell powders for our green faces.

Babes in the Wood

how am I supposed to survive in this dead land   where the light bleaches
us like driftwood   where the churches announce the hour without you
you were too green   too much an oddity   a small boy   I understand
that this land couldn't keep you   that it moved too quickly   the
light too bright   the smoke too dark   your small body fading into
bones they couldn't deny   the greenness of   if their god doesn't
want you I'll keep you   tucked into my armpits like a small green ghost
once upon a time   two children were crying in a wolfpit   how were
they to know that   they had come into a world without belonging
in it   I suppose I'm still pretending I'll find you   on my way home
curled up in a peony   tucked into the undergrowth   please   a glen
a glade a valley a crossroads   anywhere the dead might take my hand
so this bright world doesn't burn   you're my only one to remember
home with   the only one who knows our mother's whistling songs

Can't Miss What You Never Had

I had four brothers and for fun they turned themselves into lacewings. Bodies a bite of sap the size of my father's thumbnail. They collect on the dashboard of our old estate car, scrapped ten years ago. I'm afraid for them. As fine as spun sugar; they could fit into the creases of my brow. Their fire-bead eyes want to invent a mouth to laugh with. My four brothers want to tell me that they are made of magic and will live forever. Trapped in the gauze of their wings is the green air and the broad moon and my father leaning from the car to take a picture of the sky.

Lich-Wake

For The Old Croghan Man, Ireland, c. 300 BC

Croghan still twists at night

                              spends the hours trying to unclench a fist
                              knuckles wound tight as corkscrews

head / lost relic

                keeps reaching for an open seam   let me

tell you what he told me

                in the language of his apple-peel skin
                his bookend shoulders

                              he's not dead

Old Croghan is here in his sphagnum bed   and there in Dublin

he wears the restless awake

speaks the language of   a horse's whicker   a soft belly of grain
the sodden earth   the night folding down from above
                the view of the stars from Brí Eile

                         ask him through the glass

was the sky always quiet for you   did you find names for everything
how did your voice sound
                they call him old but he was young

                         yes   he says
                         your age

The Star Carr Headdresses
(red deer bone and antler, c. 9300 BC)

They picked skulls clean to wear them, danced
like the moon on top of the water. How
many years vanished like a spark from struck flint?
Somewhere, the last Irish elk died, the aurochs
retreated into myth. There are axe heads
where you can see the hands that made them.
Then the ice melts, birch turns to oak, slowly
you might uncover the name of a God, a carved
face in the rock. There's always been seals here
hiding in the estuary. Druids cut open the bellies
of hares, the wall in the North marks the furthest
reach of an empire. Even here the gods wear horns:
Cernnunos is stepping out of the woods again
and the faery courts are re-enacting the Bacchae
and the Devil is all dressed up for midsummer
with his best horns on. We are daydreamy under
the faded yellow worm moon. The red deer
go on chewing clover, the fields undulate,
the crows cackle. Where is this otherworld, where
the gods are six inches high, as numerous as ants,
and the stones creak amongst themselves? *Don't look.*
A deer shakes his human face, stands up on two legs.
We're so near, near enough to hear his laugh
the strange steps
of his dance.

Genealogy for Spiritualists

My ancestors matryoskha'd inside of me are marvelling. Robert, how do I reach you? 1855, he wrote: *When I am dead and in my grave and all my bones are rotten, take up this book and in it look that I am not forgotten.*

Grace in the bloodline fizzing like champagne, electric angels down the chimney. Years ago, Great-Grandmother saw ball lightning float through her living room, past the eggshell teacups with their astonished geishas, past Aunt Violet screaming. Past us, forever blue, marked.

Mother lets the dead cat purr round her feet. Mother meets God in her dreams, has a boyfriend possessed by the Devil. Mother was famous for being the first bottle blonde in Teesside. Once, she taught me to lie. I was seven. *You're too honest,* she said. *So lie until I believe it.*

Nana rising like Christ, her footsteps on the stairwell all slipper-shuffle, so real we could call to her and did. Those mornings she did the Lord one better. Came back twice, her ghost.

I was born with one foot backwards, already walking the backwards paths of the dead. Spiritualist Doctrine holds the dead age – the soul rewilds itself. I tell you this because when I met my brother for the first time he stood taller than me.

When my Mother was much younger than I am now and my brother's cancer etched him like a fresh copperplate, she rushed home, passing herself on the way. I like to think it was me she missed, arriving from another time to catch them.

I ought to say my Nana named everyone for her sister's dead children, each sibling already a ghost. This is the smallest branch of the tree. It blooms roses in winter, sweats amber, knows what the devil calls himself. On the day I ask where my brother is buried I will bring him a spade.

A Poem as The Goddesses Playing Mini Golf, and Pausing in Their Backswing to Look to Me and Say

"Every action in this ceremony must be performed silently *and* backwards *for only thus do we begin to walk the paths of the dead"* – Paul Huson, *Mastering Witchcraft*

you wanna speak to the dead, kiddo?   go ask your mother
she's by hole 15, throwing whale bones into the plastic
lake and arguing with your father about bitumen.

everyone's counting on you to dream him
back into the room,   easy peasy.

a few drops of the operator's blood.
you'll conjure an uncle who's also a magician,

dream of an eagle, dream of a candle.
how can a family be running towards a death
all its own? your mother, salting the door against the ghosts
of abusers. do you dare open it?

the madness is you think you can do it. poetry
as this. line break
          as god, this dark madness satin and crow feathers

like walking round a golf course backwards and silent,
          the sun rising in the west.

the body houses its bones. the smallest ossuary you know.
you're not writing the dead back to life you're just
fighting with the way your face is an obituary.

spend thirteen days and nights in prayer. or watch him spring to life
on Youtube, where the mouse is a little callous planchette
or Edison's necrophone.

I'm still one over par, by the way (they disqualified you
                              for walking backwards).

there's vervain and honey in your teeth. you've been eating
your ingredients again. bad witch; time out.

once, the dead swam freely like whales, lapping
on the shore of your mother's mind, then they got sent away.
you've spoken to every damn thing that'd listen but

the dead won't visit you,

so poetry is the gods' landline so you're reaching an answerphone
so you're playing mini golf. but he won't appear here
                              watch

Lich-Wake, Again

Not after Seamus Heaney, but certainly not before him either.

Seamus with a deck of Tarot cards, letting the night in
laying spells in the museum   American tourist
backpedalling   looking over the
skin's red vellum   inlay of fingerprints   bound tight
as stitched buckram   talk vanishes under
this small half-corpse   I begin

1. Hanged Man

A boundary stone might be used not to mark space
but instead the edge itself, I mean how a boundary is
in of itself a space and that space exists in places where
place is not a concept but rather a suggestion   what
I mean is the otherworld's zinging threshold   what
I mean is a kind of eternal life.   what
I mean is stillness

2. The Chariot

When asking a man how he died we must be aware
that the dead have no fundamental commitment to truth
while being aware that a Tarotist is pulling tongues
          out of songbirds while being aware of puppetry
regardless it seems clear to me that this was a man of war
he wanted to tell his story this young man
wanted the act of wanting again

3. Death

I asked him what he thought he said *magician*
but meant bard they did not distinguish it then
we return to boundaries the tongue of an absent head
a woman did it   turned him ceremonial
in a community by a faery hill   last meal of buttermilk
the word we're avoiding is   sacrifice

4. The Emperor

A man describes himself as a rightful king
A man describes himself as a rightful king
A man describes himself as a rightful king

An Introduction to Palmistry for Someone Seeing Their Hands for the First Time

i.

Gods can't wear watches and they can't know how badly timed they all are, but I digress. If you speak softly to the bodies of the dead, speak to them like the marsh tide rising up and down with the rain they will extend their specimen hands. Touch their lips, lingering scent of earth and sphagnum moss. Apologise for waking them.

Ever want to escape from yourself?

ii.

I meet my brother on the way home and his name is a valley for those that didn't make it out of their childhood. I think of my heartline and the airless acidity of the marsh and how I can't do anything for either of us. I confess to a bog body preserved behind museum glass that I'm afraid. I'm still looking to my palms for advice on growing up alone.

As Above So Below

The bog's backwards witchland
holds unknown anatomies, as
many as a length of string is long,
as unreachable as time's thick
molasses. Peat-swimmers.
Moss cairned. Holy red lambs.
Here is the underland. Time
is an unseeing eye, carved
Baltic amber. Here in the below
places where red bodies open
their mouths to speak:
the wool-wrapped boy offering,
the mislaid king. The horizon
a suspended anchor, body mid-
air. All time is no time: a body
is here yesterday and a hundred
years. A body here is is no body,
it breathes the amniotic of the bog.
The world tipped upsides: a sky
rootspeckled, a body occupied
in multitudes. Living spirit.
Lichenhome. A place extending
the aged branches of itself. Here
the water is a song the land is singing.
Oh harvest. Oh thinnest of days. Come
to this land, these lost days. Come
to this faery place. The hags are young
again, spinning the first story,
the first magic is falling up
into a backwards sky.

Estelle Price

Photograph: Jonathan Price

Estelle Price lives in Cheshire but can often be found on the Llŷn Peninsula, close to the sea. Estelle is the winner of the 2021 Welsh Poetry Competition and the 2018 Book of Kells Writing Competition. She writes from a feminist perspective on a range of themes including her East End past, the body, and the Bloomsbury Group. Her poetry has been placed or listed in the National, Bridport, Welshpool, London Magazine, Much Wenlock, Canterbury, Verve and other competitions. Poems have left home for *Poetry Wales, Crannóg, Marble Poetry, 14 Lines, Alchemy Spoon* and the *Stony Thursday Book.* Before she knew she was a poet she was a lawyer, a classicist, a charity worker.

behind closed doors

none of us ever knew how it began　　which word or act
would be the kindling that coaxed the embers　　that never quite
extinguished　　back into flame　　for a day or so the house
could ignore the heat　　the threat to its joists and floorboards
could pretend the fire was manageable and would stay contained
in the throat where it was lit　　always a shift came　　when the
smoky air thickened, changed colour and the Beginning gave way
to the Middle　　in the Middle two girls sat on a narrow staircase
in cotton nightdresses, plaiting and re-plaiting each other's hair
neither up nor down　　wanting their mother　　in the Middle
the walls turned inside out to get away from the noise and doors
slammed themselves to draw attention to their distress　　unlike
the Beginning, the Middle was determinate　　there was always
a stone floor the fire was too scared to cross　　(although the two
girls on the stairs did not know this)　　by the News at 10 the End
was reached as if the bells of Big Ben demanded it　　so sudden
that the house did not have time to rearrange itself　　so sudden
the fire was forced to sink to its knees　　like the Beginning, the
end of the End was unknown　　except that it was preceded by
silence　　forked through with blame and shoved into the stair
cupboard to make space for the next Beginning

Carol (and her wing girl)

Summer 1976

The heat parachutes into the playground, melts tarmac to treacle
stains the soles of her cork platform shoes. Carol, secretly tattooed

princess of the girls' loos. From the crowd of ordinary she picks
me to be her wing girl. Each recess we lean against the caretaker's

cabin. Barbie and her shadow. Her dyed blond hair,
with its hint of pink, drifts loose, sweat-free. She hitches her skirt

to tease and test, tells me what it's like to hang out at Barking station
with Danny. How he gets off on her white plastic boots

the orange cap I crocheted. She squeezes a fag between fingers
circled with rule-breaking rings, puts her arm in mine, whispers

where he likes to kiss her. Says she's going to skip games again
pretend it's her time of the month, sit in the changing room chewing gum,

her breasts cupped in a bra size I can only imagine. Twin studs
bed down in her ears, a dab of *Smitty* anoints them. Once, after school,

she fought a girl in the street. A mess of nail varnish,
blood, torn blouses and hissing. Later, she said she'd fight for me

if I wanted her to. But mostly I preferred to read. She left at sixteen
to work in a shop. I saw her once, glossed and shadowed, selling

faces on the make-up counter. We lost touch. Before long
I too was gone with my cap and gown, green hair and pretensions.

The Oxford interview

'Another Bastion Falls to Women: Oxford' by William Borders, *New York Times Nov. 11 1979*

I'm in a wood-panelled room with two dons / they are asking a question / it starts like this / *a man boards a train* / *by mistake he leaves behind his umbrella in the waiting room* / they don't say what kind of umbrella / let's assume it's a special one / let's give it a silver-topped parrot head bought from an umbrella shop on High Holborn / they continue / *he leaves the umbrella leaning against a seat* / how careless / his wife will be angry / I'm making that bit up / to be clear it's only the skeleton of the story the dons give me / *very soon another man comes along* / definitely a thin man, I can see his ribs / *he picks up the umbrella and walks off along the platform* / (this is said by the don who is blind) / what he doesn't say, but I'm sure happens, is that the thin man swings the umbrella as if it's his own / *now*, say the two dons, *your turn, is this*

theft? / it's a trick question surely? / he's half-inched it / he's probably already working out how to sell it down Rathbone market / like those starchy sheets someone in the family caught as they dropped off the back of a lorry / the ones we all smoothed over our mattresses / so I say / *yes it's*

theft / the older don looks glum / (he wants to fill this year with 'girls') / adds a supplementary / *but what if to exit the station,* (he says like it matters) *the man will have to walk past the station master's office?* / and I'm back in Boots secreting blue eye-shadow and Rimmel mascara in my pocket and putting it back on the shelves after ten minutes / just for the hell of it / remembering what Carol said / it's only stealing if you've

left the premises / so I look the don in the eye / the one who isn't blind / and I say / *it depends* / like I'm an authority / *it depends, of course on what the thin man intends* / and they smile in bearded unison / and it's a life-changing moment / a moment causally linked to five births, a divorce, six weddings / but all the way back to the bricks and mortar station / to the train that will take me to Paddington / I want to say / of course he was nicking it / didn't you see the state of his shoes? / didn't you see the ditches round his eyes? / have you forgotten there was only fluff in his wallet? / and I want to ask / why are there only men in the story? / where are the women? / until I remember that none of it is real / that what I've applied to read is law not imagination

Primigravida

Before

She was happy. Her body bubbled from its source –
a river unaffected by dams or diversions.

She had a scar on her temple since childhood –
it no longer mattered.

She thought of herself as 'possible'.

She ran like a dog let off the leash,
round the paths of Victoria Park, her legs humming.

She knew she had the right to say no
even when a prince unpinned her hair in the kitchen.

First Trimester

She was happy, or sad, each morning her belly heaved
as if trying to rid itself of the foetus.

She had a scar on her temple –
it belonged to a fairy story she couldn't remember.

She thought of herself as possessed.

She ran along the Thames as if her arms were full of boxes
husband latched to her side.

She knew her rights had changed but
she couldn't find the paragraph with the detail.

Second Trimester

She was blooming, they said. Her breasts, two
one-eyed monsters in milky dialogue with her womb.

She had a scar on her temple but no one
not even her mother, paid it attention.

She thought of herself as an experiment.

She ran awkwardly, like an unclipped dog with three legs,
close to the edge of the Regent's Canal.

She knew that rights and what was 'right'
were two different stories, in a lifetime's collection.

Third Trimester

She was bursting. Her naked body a giant plum
its wrinkled stone demanding an exit.

She had a scar on her temple. She scratched it
to make it throb like it had before.

She thought of herself as context.

She ran, in her imagination, into the river and out
the other side without getting wet.

She knew she didn't want a Caesarian but
on the day of the birth it became – necessary.

After

She is empty. Her body wants back the baby
cut out like Little Red Riding Hood from the wolf's belly.

She has a scar on her temple from where her mother
hit her when she was seven. A small hand grazes it.

She thinks of herself as riven.

She runs after six weeks, east towards Hackney Marshes,
her husband left behind with the tempest.

She is learning the knotted language of need. Longing
pulses at her wrist, hers and her daughter's.

Come night

after Derek Mahon

And why would I not wish, after a drawerful of days
disarrayed with worry, to walk into dusk's byways
leaving the back gate unlatched? Come night
I'll say, lead me away from the probing kitchen light
where fear simmers blood-orange like a dying sun
and all the talk is of treatment not yet begun.
Race me across the cropped grass until my mind
is infused with black, the future set free, undefined.
Somewhere in the forest a badger leaves the sett
to forage for her cubs. Inside a child learns the alphabet
his small hand feeding the page with words.
I stand with my back to the door knowing in spite
of everything a mother never loses the urge
to run, for who can tell if everything will be alright?

The morning after a lie was born

When we set off for Clissold Park, one stainless
Sunday morning, the lie (I know this now) was just

new-born. You'd birthed him as the full-fat moon
spurted light into a borrowed bedroom

then washed his dangling limbs in whisky fumes
and semen. Swaddled, you brought him

home at midnight. He lay between us till
the rooster cried, a red-eyed laboratory

rat intent on getting fat on rancid milk.
His mouth froth-stopped. After I'd made you

bacon and egg, you slapped the drooling
lie into the top pocket of your new-bought

Barbour jacket. Said, you'd had enough
of questions, when would I start

believing? While the lie took a nap
we walked beside the pond, threw burnt toast

to the solitary swan, whose whooping
woke the lie. Grown too leggy, already,

for the pouch in which you'd trussed him,
he dropped at your feet. Began wailing.

Argument

after Rene Magritte – 'The Month of the Grape Harvest'

The men in bowler hats
are looking through my open window.
Rows of them, massed like unlit matches,
suited and unsmiling. There are too many
eyes for me to meet, iron eyes that wait
for an apology.

My room is blue, even the skirting board.
Even my point of view, grown too big for my face,
is blue like a Forget-Me-Not or
the beginnings of a bruise.
Blue, I read yesterday, is not
the colour of compromise.

The men are still waiting.
All their closed lips are ready to bite
into my excuses. They are wearing your ties
knotted like the veins of our conversations.
If I blink, they will leap into my skin
line up round the walls
while they decide what tint
to paint my opinions.

Chains

if I had been unafraid
when you kicked us away from the kerb
sure of the saddle between my legs
laughing at each shimmy and shake
     if, with the sun overhead, I had stopped myself
     reaching for a brake that didn't exist
     when we pitched into valleys
     where all we could see was mist
       if I had been content at the corners
       to lean in your direction
         if I had not lost my footing
         as we climbed a hill of terraces
         with front doors that needed painting
         my body becoming languid
         and burdensome like a sack of bricks
         you were keen to tip into a skip
           if I had been happy to pedal at night
           through tunnels, alleys, forests and cities
           through the sex and the arguments
           the shouting and the kissing without needing
           to know where we were on the map or
           whether we had passed the road
           that led back to the beginning
             if I had known when to scream
             and when to sing
               if I had believed
               the view of your back
               was as beautiful as a Titian
                 if I had understood
                 that, for you, a tandem was an
                 exceptional gift, then
would I still be the woman
whose voice got lost in the wind
whose words were chained
to the power in your legs?

iii

after Vanessa Bell, The Tub, 1917, painting
of Mary Hutchinson, Clive Bell's mistress

I begin with three.
Circular tub, grey pitcher, Mary
leant over, her alabaster chemise hung
like a bride's veil from peachy shoulders.

A wide window reveals charcoal sky,
allows the night's curiosity to rinse the attic
in glitter. At the canvas edge a solitary
curtain flushes. Will this do?

No, begin again. There is too much pink,
too much harmony. Mary, Mary, you should
be nude for the sake of decency.
Your navel's black stone

exposed, eyes cast down,
fingers busy with plaited hair. Let's cover
the floor with bruised sand, introduce
a vacant space

between your boyish thighs. The pitcher?
Take it away. Boiling water can't dissolve
the odour of this woman's desire.
The bath must

alter. Tip it up, let it open, mutate
to a single-minded orifice that gapes at the heart
of the composition. Or is it a ring?
A hoop of wedded-metal.

Enough. I'll finish with an arched window,
an urn set on a purple sill, artist's trap for a trio
of wilted tulips, two-red-one-yellow.
I end, I always end, with three.

Safe house

It's square with book shelves that float. Light gushes although I don't know the source. In this room women come to sit, examine the wounds on their wrists. There are no windows only a yellow door between the shelves. On good days the air is warm. Fear has not fallen on the floor. There are no tears just the slow tick of words going backwards. Sometimes a glass vase has been filled with chrysanthemums. On bad days the other person in the room asks me to describe what lies behind the yellow door. I pretend I see the bright edges of laughter but I know what waits is only a huge suck of emptiness like the pause after words smashed the hall light of our first house, the void before his hands reached for my throat. In this space it is enough when quiet soaks me up, folds me into a wing-back chair. It is enough if I can stay untouched until my shadow finds a way to cut itself out of my chest.

Gallop

Beside the single track road to Ballintoy Harbour,
where mossy, pot-holed tarmac is hemmed by bushes
hung with a dazzle of red and purple pendants, a grey mare

stands alone in a sloping field. Moisture glistens skin
while all around a wispy mist gathers and shifts, nullifies
the pictures that exist outside her boundaries.

She is so perfectly still as if to move a hoof,
or even an eyelid, will cause a disconnect. From the barred gate
I mirror her cultivated calm. For how long

have I chosen not to gallop, a woman tethered
to a wooden house whose wild mane is seen by no one? If I could
I would reach into the horse's hooded eyes

persuade her to surge, vault the white-faced quiet, my arms
about her halterless neck. She would fly from field
to harbour, teach me the salted vocabulary of the sea –

how to wade through surf absorbed by its stories.
Still my grey horse doesn't move. I lift the latch,
walk forward to stand beside her in the gloom.

The Manchester interview

In a room contented by books / there's a view of a brick mill chimney from the fourth-floor window / when I look longer I see hills escaping into the horizon / the woman in the chair opposite asks a bagful of questions I can answer / until the last one / until the '*why*' / which in the tutor's accent / belongs in the folds of many histories / I pause / I don't yet understand / that to be open / to allow a telescope to examine pain's retina / is not weakness / I decide not to confide that / (as in all good fairy tales) / there are three answers to her question / I don't tell this stranger

   I am here because my mother is

dead / my mother is dead / (it is impossible to say this only once, for it to make sense) / my mother is dead / no longer able to rake a comb through my ideas / no longer, with hands on her hips, able to ask whether I wouldn't be happier in an office / turning words into Statements / spending hours pulling at my heart's evidence / arranging it into box files according to type and longevity of distress / neither do I say /

   I am here because my husband has

left / walked away dangling bits of my identity from branches in the garden / pierced balloons / or is it burnt blossom? / how after it stopped hailing I gathered the debris / kept it safe in my purse / till it brought me here / in the rain without an umbrella /

   instead I say / all my life I have

read / lived in the dolls' houses of other people's stories / at last I have a hammer / can build my own / but how to make sure the windows open? / what colour to paint the front door? / and the tutor smiles / words are let out of their cells / it is a moment causally linked to everything else.

The personality of loss

The poets are having a competition
                    to see who can write best about loss
but since loss has many expressions they start by sitting in the shade of an apple tree
        (whose crimson blossoms never come to anything these days)
        to decide what is the personality of loss.

She crosses her ankles, says true loss never makes her cry;
        it drills boreholes into the heart only to fill the cavities with cement.
He blinks, turns away, says loss can only ever be weighed in tears,
            tears that scour riverbeds into cheeks before falling
                like diamonds into the Dead Sea.

As a blackbird slowly pecks at the bark, she says loss needs to have gravitas,
        Elizabeth was right,
who cares about keys, names, even houses with front doors painted
            in a shade called *Borrowed Light*?
he butts in, says it's like that bit in the Bible about every grain of sand being precious;
        each loss is an ember ready to leap out of the grate onto the rag rug
                and burn the house down.

She leans back, looks at the waiting sky,
        says loss must be incapable of being forgotten;
in fact more than that, it must alter the loser forever,
not like a change in perspective more like the amputation of a finger or a leg.
                He says maybe,
        although if she's right there's not much of him left.
Is it possible, she asks, closing both eyes, that loss is beautiful?

Since they can't agree they stop talking for a while, lie back and watch
        the petals fall like blood-tinged snow on the grass.

The end of the Ice Age

How long I was buried
I will never know. Your weight

cold, exclusive, a great sheet
I couldn't lift, pinioned me. So thick

I forgot the meaning of light,
how my surface might be altered
by its touch.

It is true
I gave up hope.

It was as if I were Eve, returned to rib
crushed in your chest –
but you made of ice
not flesh.

Then it came to an end.
You left me, scoured, hollow
bits of you, sand and gravel, deposited
in my memory.

Alone, I exulted
in your absence, my basin
virgin again, earthy, expectant
offering its stones
to the meltwater.

I was happy
to be exposed, for seed to warm
in my crust. It did not matter

if the sun kept in shadow
what came next.

Fathima Zahra

Fathima Zahra is an Indian poet and performer based in London. Her poems have won the Bridport Prize, Wells Fest Young Poets Prize and the Asia House Poetry Slam. She has performed at festivals across the UK, including Hay, Latitude and Verve. Her debut pamphlet *sargam / swargam* (ignitionpress, 2021) was selected for the Poetry Book Society pamphlet choice.
Twitter: @zeeforzahra

Metamorphosis

'Asshole, what an asshole' you roll
the words in your mouth like hard candy.

Cuss out the senior who called you a double-
crossing bitch. Here, in the back of the madrassa

van where Umma's glare won't send your tongue
cowering. Your friend and you eye the junior

with the red lips the boys whisper about. In the dark
of your bedroom, you hold a shaking brush

to your face. Plunge your hands into the mouth
of the makeup pouch, come up with a new spell.

Raise a pair of scissors to your hair, already
short and suffering. You're trying to summon

the face of a sweeter girl. Or sexier, you don't
know yet. When you step out, something

has shifted under the abaya. Umma can't keep
track of what to pull your leg about, what ledges

to talk you down from, which boy to not lose sleep over.

Constant vigilance

The nurse rubs patterns on my arm
as they send a rover down each breast,

retreating only after scooping cells.
The violet ache. Head thrumming,

I'm waved out the sliding
doors held up by prayer and bandage.

                              I felt it in the shower this morning
                              I repeat this thrice at my screening.

                     The doctor nods as she pokes and prods.
                           Just the noise of paper crinkling.

                           Has it always looked like this?
                              How long? Does it hurt?

For two weeks I wince in front of the mirror
and ignore my pinging phone. Umma pretends

nothing's sending up her blood pressure,
she scrubs the kitchen counters clean.

At the follow-up, the doctor does a slow
reveal and does not smile. We can't tell

if I should keep holding my breath
or say *Alhamdulillah*

Venam, Venam, Venam

My tongue feels out the gap where the shaky teeth once stood   In the mirror I wince at the girl with the cropped hair and open windows in her mouth   I want Uppapa to buy me all the sandwich ice creams from the corner shop   To watch Pink Panther and skip school unless it's my birthday   I want to stay in nursery and be called princess still   For my cheese sandwiches to be cut into triangles   To play with my sister but she can't go on the PlayStation yet   I want Umma to linger at the door when I'm sick   I want to go to the hairdressers like the other girls in my class   I want the new skating shoes with the blinking lights   I want my old bed To not lose any more teeth   To keep blowing candles off everyone else's cake.

* Venam – want, in Malayalam.

Missus T

Answers well up and stay set in my throat
in Missus T's class. The Hindi teacher

with the mole on her face and red cheeks
growing redder when we mumble. Wooden ruler

a ready whip in her hands –
beating to purge the Idontknow's

from our soft bellies. I was once spared
a slap on my birthday. She smiled

as if this was a kindness. At the parent's
teacher's evening, there's a queue

snaking out of her classroom.
Missus T's wearing a sari and looks like

an oil painting of herself. Her face
made up as she croons sweetly

What do you mean?

Someone says she lost her husband
that year, Umma says she can go to hell.

Anti Bint aw Walad?

The barber
shop
I'm
sliding down the wooden crate set up for me.
Uppa's talking cricket scores and the barber's snipping my hair
too close
to my neck to see I'm blinking tears.

*

The souk
Umma's
thumbing through dresses with frills and bows
for my cousin's wedding. I'm sentenced to the pink taffeta
with three layers I'll wear like sandpaper.

*

Home
I'm wiping my nose
with her nightie and keep repeating
the word monkey-boy. Umma assures me I look pretty,
and little girls shouldn't be bothered with their hair anyway.

*

The corniche
The sun
has sucked all the yellows out
of the sky and it could be the dark,
but a little girl asks me *'Anti Bint Aw Walad?'*
I turn to Umma.

*Anti Bint aw Walad - 'Are you a girl or a boy?' in colloquial Arabic.

Culling

For my first day at the madrassa,
I wear my new floral top,
pack scraps of surahs I've learned
in the passing. They curdle in my mouth
and teachers raise my name in anger. Strike
my palms for each word stumbled like
I drag nails down God's throne.
Am asked to be dressed for prayer,
always.

The further they send their hands
down my throat, the more limbs
I sprout in the dark soil. They
speak of hells and girls who don't
cover up in the same breath
and I forget of the world's softness
beyond their claws.

Pass

Boys are passing girls apples under the desk.
It's the art of quick hands, the timed glance.

There are bets on who, when, what kind of apple.
At house parties, my friends and I recreate the latest exchange,

sit across each other on our bedroom floors,
giggle while my friends chant *go on then*

> *did you hear about the boy who hoarded apples?*
> *the girl with the butterfingers?*

Parents, held outside by the guise of a locked
door and code words in texts. Crackling voices

of boyfriends, saved under Ayeshas and Fathimas.
I, too, am waiting for my glossy apple. I have perfected

the receiving palm (a *Cosmo* masterclass).
Don't care if he catches my eye, if he remembers

my name. If he whistles after, like on the field –
ears cocked for applause.

Parent Cut, Part 1

We stayed up all night, the four of us. We watched Queen for the third time. ~~Ansha was subdued. R's being an ass again. Shirin showed us the nudes she wanted to send N. We helped her pick them like we pick outfits.~~ Ansha's mom made some French toast and crab cakes. We raided her fridge after, finished all the ice cream. ~~We tried prank calling all the boys from our class that are dumb enough to leave their numbers on Facebook. They tried asking for our names so we hung up.~~ Ooh, and then we tried on her sister's makeup. Looked like a shoal of fish, all shiny and greased up. ~~We looked like the girls you call [   ] on TV.~~ I was trying on Ansha's bridesmaid gown when you called. Everyone burst into giggles, told me I need a pushup bra. ~~I sent some photos to S and he thought I looked [   ] and that's that.~~ So yeah, just the usual.

Demeter speaks

I haven't made dumplings for your brother
since you've been gone. I pretend to iron

clothes, wonder what you must be doing
this minute. I don't know my hand without yours

tugging at it. I never wanted kids.
But I've made a life of wheedling dough

into animal faces for you. They're asking me
to move on, to remember the children I do have.

I'd rather hear the banging of the door
as you storm out to your room. The careless

laughter when your friends are over,
names of boys I catch in conversations.

I see them now, hands linked as they walk
to the market. It takes me a second before

I remember your empty chair at the dinner table.

Obhur Beach

It's like he's sprung out of our old photographs.
Khaki pants and cotton candy for hair.

There's the beach towels and spread –
plantain fritters and samosas wrapped in foil.

Vintage flasks with enough to go around.
The adults warming their hands with cups of tea

have disappeared. So has time from the air.
I'm stilettos and tax-returns-old. He doesn't

look surprised to see me. His face, still pink
under the blazing sun. His lungs – not yet ash.

He asks if I want to wade to the deep end.
I'm tall enough, I nod. Take off our slippers

and we walk the slow walk. His crow's feet
are pronounced. He huffs and his face is redder

by the minute. The wind changes song
every half hour. We look at the seagulls

like they're trying to tell us something.
His lungs are catching up. The sun

is swimming down, we inch forward
and the years hit us all at once.

Is this the smile he wore before
he collapsed in mum's arms?

What do the seagulls know?

Qurbani

Aunty prayed for sheep but was blessed with a daughter.
She watched her grow with reproach. Called her home
before Maghrib. Drew empty threats about boarding schools
if she doesn't keep her head down or stay quiet. Asks
her of the boy at the bus stand a neighbour saw her with,
changes schools when the uniform is too short for their likes.

When she turns 21, aunty start looking for shepherds to herd
her. She doesn't have to search for long. They've been hoarding
gold for the wedding day since her first birthday. The last time
aunty called home, she gloats about her son-in-law, one month
into the marriage. How he asks her to dress in white, how he's
taught her to bleat, how he keeps her safe within four walls.

*Qurbani refers to the animal (here, goat) sacrificed by a Muslim family
as ritual for Eid.

Parent Cut, Part 2

Things Shirin thinks will kill her

- Her boyfriend not texting
  back after the date she
  had to miss tuitions for
- Her mum's mood swings
- Her shade of brick red lipstick
  going out of stock

Things that might actually kill her

- Her uncle who leaks her
  WhatsApp texts
- Her father's backhand
- Her grandfather's shotgun
  he's reserved for daughters
  that will bring him shame.

Muffin

It came out of nowhere, the year I turned twelve.
Uppa thought I had worms in my belly,
that they built a congregation there.
How else do you explain this pouch
of shame. Classmates lift their salwar tops
in the summer heat to wipe off the day's shine,
I stop in my tracks like a marked animal.

For our school farewell, I ask aunty
to drape the pallu of my saree tight
ensure it stays hidden. In the changing room
at the pool, I glance at bellies.
How distended, how flat – mine fills my duas.

I imagined chopping it off, look up liposuctions,
read pamphlets for my 70-year-old uncle's tummy tuck
– picture the giddiness in the post-surgery ward

to turn up at the piercer's, a week later,
oh, to pull up my top, and say – 'Here.'

The Committee of Eldest Daughters

meet once a month if they can.
When they aren't translating birdsong
or writing letters of recommendations
for The Committee of Wavering Sons,
The Black Sheep. A kind benefactor
hears of them, sends a lifetime supply of bath bombs
and essential oils. No one's got time for love.
They remind each other to dress warm for the weather
and take their sleeping pills. They remember the moment
their mother's love for them ran short. Somewhere
an eldest daughter is crumbling in her childhood bedroom
and the ants come to feast. There's always the lover
outside the bedroom door, fist hovering, pre-knock.

Smaller hells

When I ask if the curry's hot, *try some*
mum goads. Like she didn't shriek

when the iron branded little moons
on my palms – she ironed my clothes

for the next three years. Once, after dinner,
the room still hazy with nostalgia and stale laughter,

mum's eyes bulged before her gasp. The smell
of hair singeing, a forgotten candle. She held

my sister until she fell asleep crying.
Not about the lock of burnt hair,

but what could've been. We'd grown
stepping around pre-ordained fires.

I don't carry a matchbox like Muhammad Ali did,
but my madrassa teachers summoned and named

these fires each lesson. For hairs peeking out scarves,
bared shoulders, a dirty joke. The fire dies down

in my eyes with each warning. I outgrow
those wooden benches, learn to lie

and kiss with my eyes closed.

Thanks and Acknowledgements

Kym Deyn:
There are many people who deserve the blame, rather than the thanks for these poems, including my partners-in-crime Fahad Al-Amoudi, Prerana Kumar and Jay Hulme as well as the extended Durham University Slam Team family, my darling Jordon, my parents and assorted spirits. The blame and the thanks goes to The Writing Squad, especially Stevie Ronnie, for making me a poet in the first place. Finally a huge thank you to Jane and Rishi for all their help, Linda France, Steve Dearden, The Old Croghan Man, and the poetry communities of the North that have kept me writing.

These poems, in one form or another, have appeared in *Butcher's Dog, Neon, Reliaque, Not About Now* and the Brotherton Poetry Prize anthology.

Estelle Price:
I owe so many thank yous. To: Rishi Dastidar, Jane Commane, John McCullough and students on the NWS Advanced Poetry Workshops, John McAuliffe, Vona Groarke, Bo Crowder, Peter Viggers, Roselle Angwin and the Ionistas, the Seamus Heaney Summer School, the Arvon Foundation and a particular course at Lumb Bank in 2014 where I met words properly for the first time – I've learned about the character of poetry from you all. To my Mum and Dad, who are often laughing in my memories, to my huge loving family – Alice, Joel, Theo, Alma, John, Emily, Nat, Ben, Jacob, Hannah, Lucas, Georgia, Alison, Andy, Rose, Charlie, Beth, Ant, Ivan, Bron, Ben, Fran, Dan, Sophie (you are a list poem!) for your encouragement and most of all to Jonathan, who arrived as all this was beginning, for his big love, for his belief in me as a poet.

'behind closed doors' shortlisted as part of 2020 Mairtín Crawford Award, 2019 Bridport Poetry Competition and published in *Poetry Wales*. 'Carol (and her wing girl)' was shortlisted in the

2016 *London Magazine* Poetry Competition. 'Primigravida' was commended in the 2021 Verve Poetry Competition. 'Come night' was published in *14 Lines*. 'The morning after a lie was born' was highly commended in 2016 Much Wenlock Poetry Competition. 'Chains' was published in *Poetry Wales*. 'iii' – published, 1st in 2021 Welsh Poetry Competition. 'Safe house' was Highly Commended in 2019 Ver Poetry Competition. 'Gallop' was published in *Marble Poetry Magazine*.

Fathima Zahra:

Earlier versions of 'Metamorphosis', 'Culling' and 'Qurbani' have been published in my pamphlet *Sargam / Swargam* (ignitionpress, 2021).

Many thanks to Yomi Ṣode, Maura Dooley and Claire Cox for their guidance on these poems.